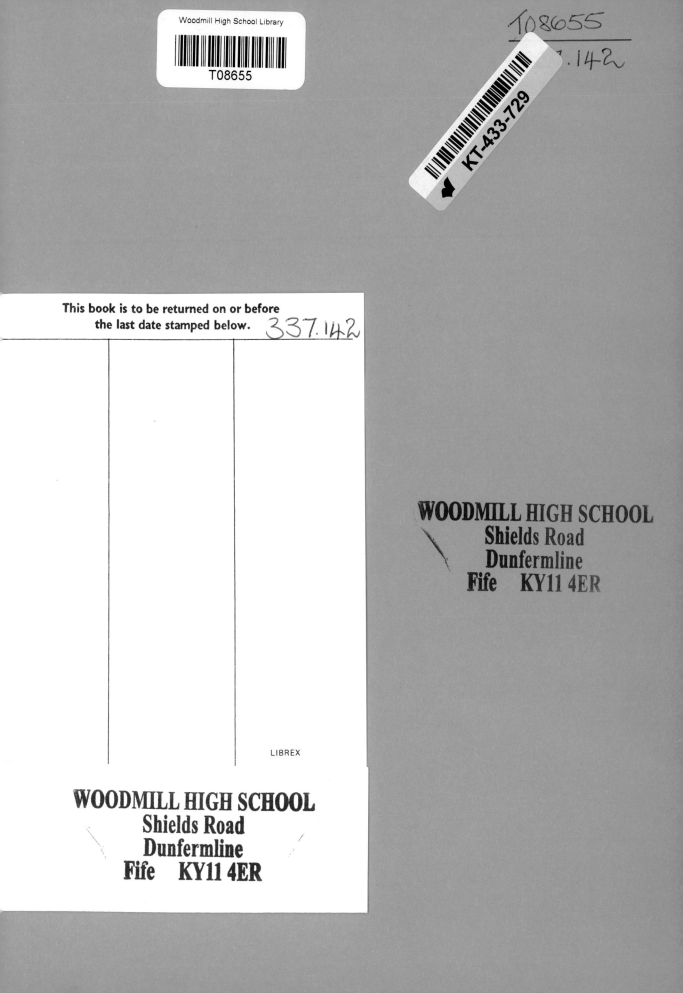

A Citizen's Guide to

The European Union

Douglas Willoughby

Revised and updated by Stewart Ross

Heinemann

H **www.heinemann.co.uk/library**
visit our website to find out more information about **Heinemann Library** books.

To order:

☎ Phone 44 (0) 1865 888112

📄 Send a fax to 44 (0) 1865 314091

💻 Visit the Heinemann Bookshop at www.heinemann.co.uk/library to browse our catalogue and order online.

First published in Great Britain by Heinemann Library, Halley Court, Jordan Hill, Oxford OX2 8EJ, part of Harcourt Education.
Heinemann is a registered trademark of Harcourt Education Ltd.

Design: M2 Graphic Design
Indexed by Indexing Specialists
Originated by Ambassador Litho Ltd.
Printed in China by WKT Company Ltd.

10 digit ISBN 0 431 06171 8
13 digit ISBN 978 0 431 06171 9

10 09 08 07 06
10 9 8 7 6 5 4 3 2 1

British Library Cataloguing in Publication Data
Willoughby, Douglas
  A citizen's guide to the European Union. - 2nd ed.
  1.European Union - Juvenile literature
  I.Title II.The European Union
  337.1'42

A full catalogue record for this book is available from the British Library.

Acknowledgements
The publishers would like to thank the following for permission to reproduce photographs: AFP/Gerard Cerles p15, Thomas Writh p19; Camera Press London/Peter Dierkes p41, Rota p43; Corbis pp10, 27; European Regional Development Fund p32; Impact/Mark Henley p4, Robert Eames p22; Northwest Development Agency p31; PA Photos/Barry Batchelor p24; Popperfoto pp6, 8,16, 21, 35, 36, 39; Rex Features pp13, 29.   EXTRA PICS

Cover photograph of The European Union flag, reproduced with permission of Getty Images/The Image Bank.
Every effort has been made to contact copyright holders of any material reproduced in this book. Any omissions will be rectified in subsequent printings if notice is given to the publishers.
The paper used to print this book comes from sustainable resources.

CONTENTS

Introduction

History of the EU

The EU's Structure and organization

The EU in action

The EU and its citizens

Any words appearing in the text in bold, **like this**, are explained in the Glossary.

INTRODUCTION
The European Union and you

Britain is a member state of the European Union (EU). As a British **citizen**, you are also a citizen of Europe. So, what does this mean?

What is the EU?

The EU consists of 25 member states with more than 454 million people living in them. The member states are Austria, Belgium, Cyprus, the Czech Republic, Denmark, Estonia, Finland, France, Germany, Greece, Hungary, Ireland, Italy, Latvia, Luxembourg, Malta, the Netherlands, Poland, Portugal, Slovakia, Slovenia, Spain, Sweden, the Netherlands and the United Kingdom. Other countries have applied to become members, and negotiations are taking place between the EU and these countries.

Because you hold the nationality of one of the member states of the EU (in your case, British), that makes you a citizen of the Union. This runs alongside your British citizenship – it does not replace it.

The European Union must prove itself relevant to the region's young people.

What does European citizenship mean?

Being a citizen of the European Union gives you certain rights:

>> You have the right to travel, live, work and study in every EU country (member state).

>> You have the right to vote and stand for election in local and European Parliament elections in your country of origin or residence.

>> You have the right to submit a petition to the European Parliament on any relevant matter and you have the services of an **ombudsman** to investigate your complaints.

>> You have the right to the diplomatic protection of the EU if travelling outside it.

How has membership of the EU changed life in Britain?

Since the United Kingdom became a member of the European Economic Community (**EEC**) in 1973, Europe has played a larger and more important part in our lives. More than ever before, British people are travelling to other European countries, to work, to study or for holidays. For the same reasons, more people from mainland Europe are travelling to Britain.

Many footballers from EU countries are playing for British teams. British firms are doing more and more business with the other member states, either by **exporting** their goods to them or by selling services such as banking and insurance. In return, an increasing selection of goods produced in the EU is available for us to buy in our shops and supermarkets.

Perhaps most important of all is the way in which laws and **directives** agreed in the EU are applied to Britain. A good example of this is The Working Time Directive. The aim of this is to make sure that the health and safety of European workers does not suffer through working excessively long hours or by not having proper rest periods. The directive provides for a maximum 48 hour working week over an agreed period, a minimum daily rest period of eleven consecutive hours, a rest break where the working day is longer than six hours, four weeks annual paid holiday and a maximum of eight hours night working. Millions of workers throughout Europe have welcomed this directive as a way of improving their lives. Some employers, but not all, dislike it. They see it as Europe dictating to them how they should run their businesses, whilst some claim that the directive itself adds to their costs and puts up prices.

This directive highlights a number of issues about Britain and the European Union. There are many who believe that European Union membership is bringing great benefits to Britain, not just in trade but also in closer political cooperation. There are also those who think that the EU interferes too much in Britain and that membership will lead to the loss of more and more of our independence.

Many people take what may be considered a 'middle view'. They are happy about increasing trade and cultural links, but less certain about closer political ties that might lead to political union of all the member states. Many do not want to be part of a 'United States of Europe', a **federal** Europe, with Britain governed not from Westminster, but from Brussels.

The fears and uncertainties of many British people about the future of Britain and the EU are highlighted by the current debate about a European **currency**, the Euro. Will Britain join? If so, when and on what terms? Will joining lead to a loss of independence for our country? These and a variety of other issues relating to Britain and the EU will be examined in this book.

HISTORY OF THE EU
Conflict and cooperation

The movement to create a union of European states has its origins in the conflicts of the first half of the twentieth century. The horrific experiences of those years help to explain why the idea of unity is so important to many people.

Nationalism and World War I

Between 1900 and 1945, Western Europe was dominated by two world wars, by the events leading to them and by their terrible consequences. **Nationalism** was a major cause of both these world wars, but is best illustrated in the events leading up to the outbreak of the First World War in 1914. During these years the leading nation states formed themselves into two alliances: Britain, France and Russia against Germany, Austro-Hungary and Italy. Because these alliances were heavily armed, they were very dangerous. The assassination of Archduke Franz Ferdinand of Austro-Hungary in Sarajevo on 28 June 1914 sparked off a series of events that ended with Britain reluctantly declaring war on Germany on 4 August.

The war itself was the most terrible in human history to that date – it was total war. **Industrialization** provided the wealth and the means to produce new weapons such as the machine gun and poison gas. These were responsible for the deaths of millions of people. When peace finally came in 1918, the countries involved began to count the cost. About ten million men had been killed in battle, and thousands of civilians had also died. Vast areas of land in France and Belgium, along with their towns, their historic buildings, factories and industries, had been destroyed. Much of German industry and farming lay in ruins, and major world economies like that of Britain had been badly damaged.

Coventry Cathedral was one of many historic buildings destroyed in the bombing raids of World War II.

Punishing Germany

In the years following 1918, members of the victorious Allies such as Britain, but particularly France, took revenge on Germany. In the **Treaty** of Versailles, Germany lost land, people and valuable mineral **resources**. The country's armed forces were drastically reduced. It was blamed for starting the war and forced to pay massive amounts of money to Britain and France to repair the damage it had caused. When Germany was unable to keep up these payments in 1923, the French invaded the Ruhr, Germany's most important industrial area. These actions by the French made millions of Germans particularly resentful, and helped to lay the seeds for the rise of the Nazis to power. Their leader, Adolf Hitler, a radical right-wing nationalist, promised the Germans that he would destroy the Versailles Treaty, rebuild and rearm Germany and make the country great again.

World War II and its aftermath

World War II began in 1939. It started mainly because Hitler, backed by his Italian ally, Mussolini, was occupying smaller countries such as Austria and Czechoslovakia – eventually he had to be stopped. Under Hitler, German nationalism had become particularly aggressive and threatened to take over Europe. When in 1945, Britain, the United States, the **Soviet Union** and their allies finally defeated Hitler, Mussolini and their Japanese allies, much of Europe lay in ruins. This was particularly true of Germany, which had to be occupied and governed by the Allies. It was also true of Poland, Hungary, the Balkan states, Italy, France, the Netherlands and Belgium, all of which had seen terrible fighting and suffering. As the people of these countries began to count the cost of war – for the second time in 25 years – they must have been wondering how long it would be before more fighting started yet again.

Beginnings of unity

With the possibility of another European war firmly in the minds of many, and the danger of **communism** spreading from the East, some politicians began to speak about the possibility of the leading nations of Europe actually working much more closely together to prevent another conflict. In a speech given in Zurich in September 1946, the British Prime Minister Winston Churchill spoke of the need to create a 'United States of Europe'. This would mean the nation states of Europe working more closely with each other to create closer economic ties and at some time in the future, a political union.

HISTORY OF THE EU
A community of nations

The idea of European unity did not begin with Churchill in 1946. It had existed since the time of the Roman Empire and was revived by the Emperor Charlemagne in the eighth century. It was, however, the destruction of Europe in World War II that made many political leaders realize the importance of closer cooperation between the nation states of Western Europe that had spent most of the first half of the century in conflict with each other – the result of aggressive **nationalism**.

Jean Monnet – 'the father of the European Community'

Although it was Churchill who made the Zurich speech calling for a closer union between the countries of Europe, it was the French businessman and statesman, Jean Monnet, who led the movement to European unity. Born in Cognac in 1888, Monnet helped to organize Allied supply operations in World War I. Between 1919 and 1923 he served as Deputy Secretary General of The League of Nations and Adviser to the Allies in World War II. In 1947, he realized that the nation states of Europe could no longer act alone, and so he began to develop the idea of a 'United States of Europe'. He proposed the formation of The European Coal and Steel Community in 1950 and who served as its president between 1952 and 1955. He also set up The Action Committee for a United States of Europe and led it as president between 1956 and 1975. In 1957, he led the creation of The European Atomic Energy Community and the **Common Market**. He died in 1979.

Jean Monnet (left) and Robert Schuman in 1952.

Robert Schuman and The European Coal and Steel Community

On 9 May 1950, in a speech inspired by Monnet, the French Foreign Minister, Robert Schuman (1886–1963) proposed that France, the **Federal** Republic of Germany and any other country wishing to join them should pool their coal and steel **resources**. This proposal, expanded through the work of Monnet himself, led to the creation of The European Coal and Steel Community (ECSC) in Paris in 1951. The ECSC **Treaty** signed in 1952 agreed to the French and German coal and steel industries being placed under a joint authority. Although Schuman later became the leader of the European movement and President of the European Parliament, he fell from power in France when his countrymen rejected his plan for a European Defence Force, because they thought it would lead to a revival of German military power. It is clear that whilst economic and industrial cooperation was possible between France and Germany, military cooperation at this stage was out of the question.

The EU and the Treaty of Rome

On 23 October 1954, following a conference in London, a modified Brussels Treaty was signed and The Western European Union came into being. In 1955, meeting at Messina in Sicily, the Foreign Ministers of France, Germany, Italy, the Netherlands, Belgium and Luxembourg agreed to integrate all branches of their economies, and in 1957 these six nations signed the **Treaty of Rome**. As well as setting up The European Atomic Energy Community, the treaties also established The European Economic Community (**EEC**), commonly known as The Common Market. Britain decided to stay out of the EEC and instead set in motion the creation of the European Free Trade Association as an alternative. The Common Market began officially on 1 January 1958 – how would it develop in the years to come?

FIND OUT... 🔍 >>

The official web site of the European Union includes all sorts of information about the EU, including its history. You can find it at europa.eu.int

HISTORY OF THE EU
A developing European Community

Following its creation, the Community developed rapidly. **Customs duties** on trade in manufactured goods between member states were reduced and eventually abolished in 1968, and a common external **tariff** introduced. The Common Agricultural Policy (CAP), which will be explained later (see page 20), was introduced in 1962. In 1961, the Republic of Ireland applied for membership, and Denmark and the United Kingdom requested negotiations with a view to joining. At a press conference held in January 1963, President De Gaulle of France announced that he would **veto** the United Kingdom's admission to the Community. Clearly, he regarded Britain's membership as a threat to the influence of France. In the same year, France and

Germany signed a **Treaty** of Cooperation. De Gaulle obviously saw a future Europe being dominated by France and Germany with Britain excluded.

Britain joins

In 1970, following the resignation of De Gaulle one year earlier, negotiations began between the European Community and four prospective new members: Denmark, Ireland, Norway and the United Kingdom. The negotiations proved successful, and on 23 January 1972, these four new members signed the Treaty of Accession. Norway withdrew in September following a **referendum**. Conservative Prime Minister Edward Heath, who was a strong pro-European, signed for the United Kingdom,

Edward Heath had led the unsuccessful British negotiations in 1963, so taking the United Kingdom into the Community in 1973 was a great personal triumph.

which became a full member of the EEC on 1 January 1973.

There was, however, considerable opposition in Britain to membership of the European Community. Many believed that the Community would come to have more control over our lives, and that the UK Parliament would have less. This, they argued, would lead to the loss of more and more of the freedom and independence of British **citizens**. Opposition to membership stretched across the two main political parties, but was particularly strong within the Conservative Party, even though Edward Heath himself was passionately pro-Europe.

Britain and the growing European Community

Since 1973, the United Kingdom has become increasingly involved in the European Community. In 1979, the European Monetary System for closer **monetary** cooperation between the member states began to operate, and the first direct elections to the European Parliament were held. Greece was admitted membership in 1981, which now stood at ten states. In 1986, at Luxembourg, these ten states signed 'The Single European Act' which came into force on 1 July 1987. This set up a **single market** where goods, people, services and money could move freely without barriers. In the same year, Spain and Portugal became Community members. The **Maastricht Treaty** of 1992 turned the EEC into the EU. This increased the cooperation between the member states to cover issues such as foreign and security policy, justice and home affairs.

The treaty also established the idea of EU citizenship. Austria, Finland and Sweden became EU members in 1995, bringing the membership to a total of fifteen countries.

Further enlargement and the future

Over the last ten years, the EU has focussed on three major issues: enlargement, the Euro and the Constitution. Following the end of communism in Europe, the Union prepared for the membership of many East European states. Accepting conditions set out in the Treaty of Amsterdam (1997) that they shoud be free and democratic, in 2004 Cyprus, the Czech Republic, Estonia, Hungary, Latvia, Lithuania, Malta, Poland, Slovenia and Slovakia all joined the EU.

Two years earlier, in January 2002, twelve member states (the Euro area) had replaced their individual currencies with a common European currency, the Euro. The experiment has not been a complete success. Major European nations, such as France and Germany, have not been able to stick to rules laid down by the European Central Bank, and Britain has become more sceptical about adopting the Euro.

Even more alarming to the European project was public reaction to the EU Constitution that grew out of the 2001 Treaty of Nice. Completed in 2004, the Constitution consolidated all existing EU treaties and agreements but could not come into force until agreed upon by all member states. Twelve countries went ahead with ratification but referendums in France and the Netherlands rejected the treaty. By late 2005, the future of the Constitution was in serious doubt.

THE EU'S STRUCTURE AND ORGANIZATION
The European Parliament

As a **citizen** of Europe, the EU affects many aspects of your life. Quite a lot of the time, you are unlikely to be aware of this! A vast number of regulations, for example, establish a high standard of quality in the food that we eat. Facilities that we use, the redevelopment of our deprived urban areas and educational opportunities that come your way may owe their origins to the EU. Given that the role and responsibilities of the EU are so complex and far reaching, it is not surprising that the organization that enables it to carry out its work is very carefully and precisely structured. It is underpinned by democratically elected representatives of the member states.

Members of the European Parliament

The European Parliament is the only body of the European Union elected democratically by the citizens of its member states. The Members of the European Parliament (MEPs) are elected for a period of five years. The first elections took place in 1979 and the most recent in 2004. There are currently 732 MEPs in total. The number of MEPs depends on the size of the population of each member state. However, this is not exactly proportional to the population. For example, one MEP from Germany represents around 828,000 citizens, while an MEP from Luxembourg represents 71,500 citizens. MEPs sit in multinational, European political groups. There are currently seven political groups in the European Parliament and 29 independent members.

The European Parliament meets in full session in Strasbourg for one week each month. In between, members meet in mini sessions and in committees in Brussels. At the beginning, the European Parliament was just a **consultative** body. However, since the **Maastricht** (1992), **Amsterdam** (1997) and Nice (2001) **Treaties**, its powers have

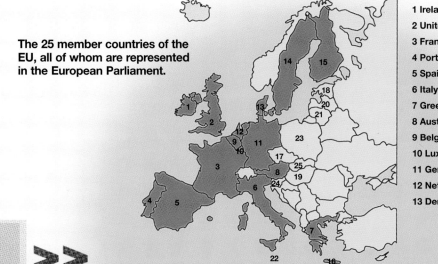

The 25 member countries of the EU, all of whom are represented in the European Parliament.

1 Ireland	14 Sweden
2 United Kingdom	15 Finland
3 France	16 Cyprus
4 Portugal	17 The Czech Republic
5 Spain	18 Estonia
6 Italy	19 Hungary
7 Greece	20 Latvia
8 Austria	21 Lithuania
9 Belgium	22 Malta
10 Luxembourg	23 Poland
11 Germany	24 Slovenia
12 Netherlands	25 Slovakia
13 Denmark	

increased and, along with the **European Council**, it now passes laws on a range of issues such as education, health and the environment. The Parliament also agrees the EU annual **budget**, currently set at around 106 billion **Euros** per year.

MEPs have a great deal of power in deciding who should be appointed to important positions in the EU. The President and all members of the **European Commission** need the approval of the Parliament before they can take office.

FIND OUT...

The European Parliament exists to represent the views of all the people of Europe when decisions about Europe are being made. These decisions have a direct impact on our lives.
Do you think it is important to vote in European elections? Why? Why not?
Can you suggest what might be done to increase the turnout in European elections? Should voting be compulsory? Why? Why not?
Should the powers of the European Parliament be increased? Would this mean reducing the powers of national governments?

Life for MEPs

Richard Corbett was elected MEP by proportional representation to represent Yorkshire and Humberside in 1996. He spends most of his week in Brussels (or Strasbourg) and returns to his **constituency** on Thursday. He spends the rest of the week and the weekend meeting **constituents** and attending meetings in his constituency. For one week in each month, Richard is in Strasbourg, attending a full meeting of the European Parliament. He spends two weeks of the month attending committees in Brussels, and the remaining week is set aside for meetings of the political groups. Most of the work of the European Parliament is carried out in specialist committees covering a particular area of EU activity – Richard, for example, is on committees dealing with economic and constitutional matters. Here, he examines draft laws and questions members of the European Commission and **civil servants** about their policies.

The European Parliament meets in this purpose-built building in Strasbourg in France.

THE EU'S STRUCTURE AND ORGANIZATION

What is the European Commission and what does it do?

The **European Commission** is made up of 25 commissioners, one from each member state. They are appointed by the government of their home country and need to be approved by the European Parliament. They are appointed for five years and they represent the EU as a whole. Each commissioner is responsible for a certain area of EU policy. The commissioners are assisted by a huge body of **civil servants** (about 25,000) who look after the administration of the Commission. Many of these are translators and interpreters. The commissioners have considerable powers, which include the following:

>> They can introduce laws and make proposals to the Council of the European Union and the European Parliament

>> They have the power to carry out agreed policies

>> They ensure that the member states and others (for example, companies) abide by the **treaties**.

Each member of the European Commission is responsible for a particular area of European policy. These are the main areas in which the commissioners work:

>> Relations within the institutions of the EU, including relations with the Parliament and managing the EU **budget**

>> Economics, including taxation

>> Business, including competition and trade

>> Transport and energy

>> Agriculture, fisheries and rural development

>> The information society, including the Internet

>> External relations and enlargement of the EU

>> Development and humanitarian aid

>> Education and culture

>> The environment

>> Justice and home affairs

>> Employment.

From this list, you can see that there is a European Commissioner working in almost all the areas that the national government works in.

Peter Mandelson – the UK's European Commissioner

Britain, along with every other member state, provides one EU Commissioner. In 2004, Prime Minister Tony Blair appointed his Labour ex-colleague, Peter Mandelson, to the vitally important position of European Commissioner for Trade. The job involves overseeing trade between the EU, the world's largest market, and the rest of the world. In particular, it means conducting delicate negotiations with other governments.

In many ways Mandelson's background had prepared him for his present task. Born in 1953 into a political family, he studied at Oxford University, then worked briefly in Africa, with the TUC, and in TV before becoming involved in politics full-time. He became an MP in 1990. However, his two spells in the Cabinet – as Secretary of State for Trade and Industry then as Secretary of State for Northern Ireland – were both cut short by resignation following accusations of misconduct. In 2005 he faced his first serious challenge as Trade Commissioner when a row erupted between the EU and China over the import of cheap clothing into Europe. The thorny problem tested to the full Mandelson's notable skills as a negotiator.

FIND OUT...

Peter Mandelson was appointed Trade Commissioner by Tony Blair, a long-standing friend and colleague. Do you think it right that a Prime Minister has such powers of patronage? Should Commissioners be directly elected? Would an elected Commissioner carry more weight in negotiations with other states?

There is more comment and information on the Commission at
http://europa.eu.int/comm

The BBC offers a brief profile on Peter Mandelson at
http://news.bbc.co.uk/1/hi/uk_politics/3916089.stm

Peter Mandelson has been European Commissioner for Trade since 2004.

THE EU'S STRUCTURE AND ORGANIZATION

What is the Council of Ministers and what does it do?

The Council of the European Union, or the Council of Ministers as it is often called, represents the interests of the member states. It is made up of ministers from the 25 member states. Which minister attends depends on the agenda. If the subject for discussion is farming, then the 25 Ministers of Agriculture meet. Ministers for Foreign Affairs attend the General Affairs Council and deal with external relations. Each minister is politically **accountable** to his or her national Parliament. The Presidency of the Council rotates between the member states every six months.

Under the various **treaties** setting up the EU, the Council of Ministers has been given a number of responsibilities:

>> Acting with the Parliament to produce new EU law

>> Co-ordinating member states' economic policies

>> Making agreements between the EU and other states and organizations

>> Working with the Parliament to set the EU budget

>> Trying to co-ordinate member states' foreign and defence policies.

>> Assisting common action on legal and police matters across the EU.

European leaders pose for a picture together in 2004.

The Council is therefore the EU's main decision-making body, implementing measures put forward by the Commission. Decisions are taken **unanimously** in the areas of common foreign and security policies, justice and home affairs. In other areas such as agriculture, decisions are taken by **Qualified Majority Voting** (QMV). Under this system, votes are allocated as follows: Germany, France, Italy, UK, 29 each; Spain, Poland, 27 each; Netherlands, 13; Belgium, Czech Republic, Greece, Hungary, Portugal, 12 each; Austria, Sweden, 10 each; Denmark, Ireland, Lithuania, Slovakia, Finland, 7 each; Cyprus, Estonia, Latvia, Luxembourg, Slovenia, 4 each; Malta, 3.

What does the General Secretariat do?

The Council is assisted by a General Secretariat, which prepares the work of the Council and makes sure that it runs smoothly. Based in Brussels, the Secretariat is headed by Secretary-General, High Representative for the Common Foreign and Security Policy, Javier Solana. Solana is assisted by Deputy Secretary-General, Pierre de Boissieu, who runs the General Secretariat. The main work of the General Secretariat is to prepare the meetings of the European Council, the EU Council and its other bodies. It advises the President and the Secretary-General on their work of coordination. It also organizes translation for meetings, meeting documents and reports of meetings, and provides legal advice for the Council and controls the Council budget.

Intergovernmental Conferences (IGC)

Intergovernmental Conferences are meetings between governments of the member states, usually on major issues. The IGC is additional to and outside the institutions of the EU. The first conference in 1950–51 set up the EU, or the European Economic Community, as it was then known. Recently, the IGC has been concerned with the EU's controversial Constitution.

FIND OUT... >>

What are your views on QMV (qualified majority voting)? Why do you think it was introduced? What are its advantages and disadvantages?

If the EU is to be enlarged by bringing even more countries into its membership, how might this affect QMV in the future?

Will enlargement also mean a larger General Secretariat with more officials?

You can find out more about the different arguments on Europe in newspapers and their online editions. the *Daily Telegraph* (www.telegraph.co.uk) is often opposed to the influence of European institutions. The *Independent* (www.independent.co.uk) is usually more sympathetic towards Europe.

THE EU'S STRUCTURE AND ORGANIZATION
What is the Court of Justice and what does it do?

From its early beginnings in the **Treaties** of Paris and **Rome**, the six founding member states of the European Community and those who later joined them have always laid great emphasis on law. Thus, over the years, the idea of Community law has grown. Community law is independent of the law of the member states and superior to it. It applies to all the member states, but like all legal systems, it needs an effective system to support it. The European Court of Justice provides this system. The judges who sit in the Court of Justice must make sure that Community law is applied uniformly in each member state, and that it is always identical for everyone in all situations. To achieve this, the Court of Justice hears disputes between member states and between individuals.

The Court of Justice is made up of 25 judges (although they rarely all sit at the same time) and eight advocates-general, who are appointed by the member states. They are chosen from judges with a high reputation for independence. They serve for a term of six years, but this can be renewed. The judges select one of their members to be President of the Court for a renewable term of three years. The advocates-general assist the judges in their work by giving impartial opinions (opinions that never favour one side or the other) on cases before the Court. Often, the judges sit in groups of three or five and hear cases brought before them. These could include:

>> Actions brought by member states against other member states

>> Actions for **damages** against the Community

>> Rulings on how Community law is interpreted

>> Actions for failure to act – against, for example, the Commission.

The Court of Justice was set up in 1952 and since then it has heard more than 12,900 cases. By 1978, 200 new cases were being brought each year – by 2003, the figure was 600. To cope with the burden of this growing number of cases, The Court of First Instance was set up in 1989. This Court is made up of fifteen judges appointed by the member states to serve for a renewable term of six years. The judges in this Court select one of their members to be President. There are no permanent advocates-general in this Court.

Right: The European Court of Human Rights in session in 2001.

>>

Human rights

What are **human rights**? A simple definition is that they are the values or beliefs that ensure a human being's individual welfare. Human rights are a relatively new idea, and the need to protect them has become more important since the horrors of World War II. In 1950, 21 countries forming the **Council of Europe** signed the European Convention of Human Rights (ECHR), promising to protect basic human rights and freedoms. Although the member states of the EU signed up to the ECHR, it is completely separate from the EU and is not a part of the EU treaty.

In the early years of the EU, greater emphasis was placed on economic rights, particularly the rights of workers to move freely around Europe. More recently, increasing emphasis has been placed on political rights such as the right to vote and to petition the European Parliament. In 1996, the European Commission proposed that the ECHR should be made part of EU law. So far, this has not happened, and there is still a great deal of argument about whether or not it should. In 1997, the **Treaty of Amsterdam** made a clear commitment to human rights. Protection from **discrimination** was extended beyond sex discrimination or that based on nationality, and the EU now has the power to impose penalties on member states for breaches of basic human rights.

Whether the EU states decide to adopt a **Charter of Fundamental Human Rights**, or to rely on the ECHR does not concern British citizens too much as the UK's Human Rights Act of 1998 incorporated the European Convention on Human Rights into British law. This means that, whatever the EU says, rights are legally protected in the UK.

European Court of Human Rights

Council of Europe

THE EU IN ACTION
The impact on farming

As **citizens** of the European Union, we have to understand that, although the British government is involved in negotiating agreements, it is no longer in complete control of all areas of the economy. Our oldest industries – farming and fishing – have been subject to **EEC** laws and regulations. These industries have therefore felt the impact of policies that were drawn up with the intention of bringing prosperity to all the member nations. The policies have been controversial with British farmers and fishermen, because many of them feel that membership of the Community has not benefited them at all.

The Common Agricultural Policy (CAP)

The Common Agricultural Policy (CAP) is a system set up to support farming in the European Union. It was established by the **Treaty of Rome** in 1958 and came into operation in 1962. For many years it was the main Community policy, initially taking up over two-thirds of its **budget**. It has provided vast **subsidies** for farmers in order to achieve its five aims. These were:

>> To increase productivity

>> To create a fair standard of living for farmers

>> To keep the markets for farm products stable – no big price changes

>> To ensure regular supplies of food

>> To ensure reasonable prices for **consumers**.

Its function is based on three principles:

>> A **single market** in farm products, with guaranteed prices and **tariff** free movement within the Community

>> Community preference – that is, a tariff system of **import** taxes and **export** refunds on trade with EU non-members

>> Shared responsibility for costs amongst all member countries.

Why has the CAP been so controversial?

>> Farm subsidies helped to keep prices stable, but this also involved dumping large quantities of excess produce that would have lowered prices had it reached the market. To buy up this produce and store it, the EU used tax-payers' money. 'Wine lakes' and 'butter mountains' became a much-publicized feature of this process of storing the excess produce. Alternatively, the EU sold the excess food cheaply to poorer countries outside the Union, but upset the market suppliers of these countries in the process. European consumers were no longer able to benefit from lower prices when production levels rose. The prices of agricultural produce increased and remained at high levels.

>> When Britain was applying for EU membership, it had to agree to abandon many of its **Commonwealth** trading links and to be supplied with food from the EU. This is thought to have significantly increased the cost of food to the British consumer.

>> Business people claim that the CAP means efficient farmers subsidize inefficient ones. This is said to be especially hard on Britain, the largest single contributor to the CAP, whose farms are generally well run.

>> Opponents of the CAP say it is not right that, after the accession of ten new members in 2004, 80 per cent of its budget is still spent in the fifteen pre-2004 states.

>> In 2005, Prime Minister Tony Blair objected that 40 per cent of the total EU budget, the proportion taken up by the CAP, was being spent on only five per cent of the EU's population.

>> Environmentalists believe that by encouraging high production at all costs, the CAP is responsible for massive environmental damage right across Europe.

>> The EU's '**set aside**' policy – paying farmers not to farm up to 35 per cent of their land – has been criticized for distorting the market in agricultural products. Environmentalists, on the other hand, approve heartily of set aside.

Recently, the CAP has been reformed to cut entirely the link between subsidy and production. Farmers are now regarded more as 'stewards of the countryside' and receive an annual lump sum (the 'single farm payment') on condition they meet certain requirements, such as maintaining hedgerows and drainage. Even so, the CAP remains controversial as Britain seeks to cut the subsidies paid to those who benefit most from the system, particularly the French.

French farmers take to the streets demonstrating about low beef prices.

THE EU IN ACTION
Farming in the north-west of England – a case study

Wyre is a district of Lancashire situated between the Fylde Coast and the lower slopes of the Pennines. Its economy is based largely on farming and on fishing at the port of Fleetwood. As in many areas of Britain, the farming industry in the region was facing difficulties before Britain entered the European Community. Prices had fallen due to over-production. Lack of money made it difficult for farmers to **diversify** into production of other types of farm produce, for example, 'farmhouse' cheeses and yoghurts. The region is, however, a popular tourist area, so some farmers began to look into other areas, such as bed and breakfast and leisure facilities.

Cattle farms, like this one in Snowdonia, in Wales, were hard hit by the ban on beef exports since the BSE crisis began.

The impact of the EU in Wyre

As dairy farming was an important feature of the area, farmers at first benefited from guaranteed prices on milk imposed by the CAP. Similar guarantees on cereals encouraged some farmers to change to cereal crops. However, the review of CAP spending in the early 1980s changed the situation. Savings had to be made, so dairy farmers were given **quotas** for milk production. In Wyre, this had serious effects. The National Farmers Union (NFU) estimated that in Lancashire, dairy farm incomes dropped by ten per cent as a result of quotas. This reflected the national trend. The threat of the extension of quotas to cereal crops and the '**set aside**' policy being imposed further undermined confidence in the farming industry in Wyre. The knock-on effect of this was a drop in the value of farmland – another blow for farmers who had been encouraged to borrow money in order to invest in development, at a time when prices were guaranteed by the CAP.

Like farmers all over Britain, those in Wyre continued to be affected by the fall in farm income as a result of the **exchange rate**. Besides keeping prices high, the strength of the pound also reduced the amount received by farmers in **subsidies** as these were paid in **Euros**. This is one area of the British economy, therefore , that might be helped if the UK adopted the Euro.

The British beef export ban

The response of the EU to the outbreak of the disease BSE in British cattle is an example of how the EU can intervene and impose its terms and restrictions on British farming. In 1995, Britain's overseas market in beef earned £650 million. This market was destroyed on one day – 20 March 1996. British beef became a cause for concern because of a disease called BSE or 'Mad Cow Disease'. A ban on British beef was imposed, and the **European Commission** immediately began to negotiate the conditions that would enable it to be lifted.

UK land taken out of production by EU 'set aside' policy

Year	Percentage of total farmland	Number of hectares
2001	10	500,000
2003	10.5	550,000
2005	7	400,000*

Source: Approximate figures from Environment Agency website

In June 1996, Great Britain and the European Commission drew up the Florence Agreement. This set out five conditions for the lifting of the ban:

>> A selective slaughter programme

>> A system for identifying and tracking the movement of animals

>> Regulations defining the content of foodstuffs from animals

>> No animals of over 30 months to be used for foodstuffs

>> All suspect parts of animals (such as brain, spinal cord) to be destroyed.

Some of the outcomes of EU action included:

>> 75,000 cattle born between 1989 and 1993 and reared with cattle suffering from BSE were slaughtered

>> Potentially contaminated animal feed was removed from farms

>> Cattle 'passports' were introduced to identify cattle born in the UK for export

>> All calves born after 1 August 1996 to BSE infected cows were slaughtered

>> A computerized system to trace cattle born after September 1998 in the UK.

Before the **export** ban, the countries of the EU were the main buyers of British beef. Although BSE had a devastating effect, cases occurred in only one third of Britain's adult breeding herds. Although it took some time for confidence to be restored and the process is not yet complete, the crisis left Britain with some of the highest food safety standards in the world.

THE EU IN ACTION
The impact on the fishing industry

Britain's other long established industry is fishing. This has also felt the impact of EU policies.

What is the Common Fisheries Policy (CFP)?

This policy originated around 1970 and underwent major reform in 2003. It is based on the principle that fish are a natural and mobile resource and so are common property – they 'belong' to everyone. The **treaties** creating the Community stated that there should be a common policy in this area, with rules accepted and followed by all member states. However, to make sure that smaller boats could continue to fish close to their homeports, a coastal band (a twelve mile limit) was reserved for local fishermen. In 1976, the member states

agreed to extend their rights from 12 to 200 miles from their shores. This effectively meant that countries could 'trespass' into the traditional fishing grounds of other member states. They also agreed that the Community was best placed to manage fisheries, so the CFP was born (1983). One of its main aims was to conserve fish stocks by setting maximum quantities that can be caught each year, known as Total Allowable Catches (TACs). By the 21st Century, the CFP was clearly failing as stocks of once plentiful fish, such as cod, fell to near-extinction levels. Reforms introduced in 2003 attempted to police European fishing more closely in order to stabilize and then reverse this situation. Governments were forbidden to subsidize boat construction and modernization, for example, and a new Community Fisheries Control Agency was established.

The European flag is burnt by fishing protestors at Plymouth in Devon. Fishermen staged this protest against the Common Fisheries Policy.

Fishing in Fleetwood

Fleetwood in Lancashire was one of the most important centres of Britain's fishing industry. It thrived between the 1940s and the early 1950s when fishing was one of the world's fastest growing food industries. The town's decline began in the late 1950s, as the figures for fish landings reveal. This followed a twelve-mile and then a 200-mile limit being imposed by Iceland – that is, fishermen were only allowed to fish 200 miles from the coast of the country. This almost totally excluded Fleetwood trawlers from their traditional fishing grounds. The subsequent decline was not helped by Britain's entry into the European Community. The imposition of the CFP and the adoption by the EC of the 200-mile limit in 1976 also brought competition from other European trawlers. Indeed, UK fishermen complained that non-UK vessels were allowed to catch more fish in UK waters than they were. This, along with the conservation quotas of the CFP, sent the industry into a downward spiral. Investment declined and trawler owners found it increasingly difficult to borrow money to improve or update their boats and equipment. The resulting unemployment has not only affected fishermen, but also onshore jobs in Fleetwood associated with the industry.

A reduced fishing industry survives. Much of this is concerned with fish that is landed elsewhere and taken to Fleetwood for preparation and processing. Fleetwood's fishing heyday is past. Some of its waterfront areas have been redeveloped to provide leisure facilities.

Fleetwood: Total landings of fish 1956-1985		
5 year period	Tonnes	Percentage change
1956-60	278,917	-9.8
1961-65	222,167	-20.3
1966-70	215,353	-3.1
1971-75	190,231	-11.7
1976-80	105,383	-44.7
1981-85	44,200	-58.1

Source: Fleetwood Fish Merchants' Association

The Cornish fishing industry

In contrast to the North Sea fisheries, the fishermen of Cornwall have weathered the CFP storm more easily. The county, with its long tradition of individual enterprise, has always relied less on large-scale business than elsewhere. Consequently, the Cornish town of Newlyn is today home to England's largest fishing fleet. Locals put their success down to a number of factors. The wide range of fish available off the south west peninsula is one, as is the careful way the mariners have conserved stocks. Unlike some fishermen, they regularly consult with experts from the International Council for the Exploration of the Sea to see what species can be safely caught. The future may be uncertain, but for the present, the CFP seems to be benefitting the fishermen of Cornwall.

THE EU IN ACTION
The single market

From its beginnings, the creation of a single, or common, internal market was the main purpose of the 1957 **Treaty of Rome**. As early as 1951, the six European states that signed the European Coal and Steel Community Treaty turned their attention to forming a wider customs union. This was the beginning of the idea of a **single market**. What does this mean? The main features of a single market are:

>> A common external **tariff** against goods **imported** from outside

>> The abolition of internal **customs duties**

>> The removal of barriers to competition

>> Freedom of movement for persons, goods, services and capital

>> The adoption of a common agricultural policy.

The customs union was complete by 1968, but for the next fifteen years, progress towards a single market was slow. Truck drivers crossing **EEC** borders still needed to produce up to 70 forms, and rates of Value Added Tax (VAT) and duty between member states often varied a great deal. Product standards and professional qualifications were not common, and industries were often confined to their own member state.

In 1985, backed by Margaret Thatcher, the British European Commissioner, Lord Cockfield, produced a report listing the weaknesses of the single market – the reasons why progress had been so slow. At about the same time, Frenchman Jacques Delors became **European Commission** President. He supported the Cockfield proposals to make the single market more efficient. In particular, he favoured the idea of **Qualified Majority Voting** in the Council of Ministers so that decisions could be made more quickly. Delors and Cockfield threw themselves into reviving the single market. They produced 282 **directives** and regulations, of which over 90% had been passed by the Council of Ministers, and nearly 80% were being put into use in the member states by the end of 1992.

Delors was particularly keen to see the single market develop further. He wanted to see the end of **passport controls** between states, the introduction of a single European **currency**, greater police cooperation and more movement of individuals across national boundaries. Some of the EU directives issued to achieve a single market seem petty and far too detailed. They refer to such items as the size and shape of vegetables and some fruit (the ideal length of a banana, for example!). They are often very irritating and are heavily criticized as examples of unnecessary EU bureaucracy and interference. In spite of this, the single market has developed quickly over the last fifteen years and there is plenty of evidence of it in our lives:

>> Hundreds of lorries from different European countries can be seen on our motorways delivering goods from EU countries

>> A wide variety of food and wines from Europe can be purchased in our shops and supermarkets

>> More British people than ever before live and work in other countries in the EU

>> More British people than ever before travel to the EU for holidays and visits.

>> It is easier than ever before for people from the member states of the EU to work and live in the United Kingdom.

Eurostar trains run a regular service through the Channel Tunnel between the UK and France.

The European Economic and Social Committee (ESC) of the EU is a non-political body that oversees the workings of the single market. It is the voice of millions who work in the single market – for example, business organizations and **trade unions**. Its opinions are passed directly to the Council of Ministers, the Commission and the European Parliament. It was set up by the 1957 Treaty of Rome to work for the greater social and economic integration of the **Common Market.**

The ESC has 317 members, the size of the state's contingent being roughly proportionate to its size. They belong to various groups: employers, trade unions, workers and consumers. The ESC's main task is to suggest policy on social and economic matters. This clearly includes the working of the single market. In fact, on some issues, the ESC has to be consulted by the Commission and the Single European Act, and the **Maastricht Treaty** increased the number of these issues. As the single market develops, the ESC is increasing in influence and importance.

THE EU AND ITS CITIZENS
The diverse people of Europe

You are a **citizen** of Europe simply because you are a citizen of the United Kingdom, one of the member states of the EU. The same is true of all the citizens of Europe. All are different because of their customs, traditions and the language they speak. Member states have different needs and priorities. Some are poorer than others or have areas of economic decline and deprivation. Some member states have distinctive, regional differences inside the country itself, sometimes based on religious or ethnic differences from the past (in Ireland, for example). In others, these differences are so noticeable that these regions could almost be separate states in their own right. In some European countries, wars and **treaties** have brought together people of different origins and lifestyles under one nation state. This applies to regions of Belgium and Germany, to Catalonia and the Basque country in Spain, or to Scotland and Wales in the UK. The EU recognizes these regional differences and is committed to establishing **cohesion** (more equal levels of prosperity between the regions of the member states).

As the EU grows in size, it is increasingly important to ensure that everyone is aware of the benefits of belonging, whilst at the same time keeping their own identity. There is, therefore, a conscious effort to encourage a sense of belonging to this larger union called Europe. Much of this work is carried out through the **Committee of the Regions**. Financial support is provided by what are called the Structural Funds. There are four of these funds, but perhaps the most significant is the European Regional Development Fund (ERDF).

The Committee of the Regions and the Bureau

The **Maastricht Treaty** in 1992 established the Committee, and the **Treaty of Amsterdam** in 1997 extended its areas of action. The most important of these are:

>> Economic and social unity

>> Health, education and culture

>> Employment policy, **single market**, and economic policy

>> Social policy, health, consumer protection, and tourism

>> Agriculture, rural development, and fisheries

>> **Vocational** training, education and sport

>> Transport and communications across Europe

>> Fundamental **human rights**.

There is a Commission for each of these areas. Like the ESC, the Committee itself has 317 members, who are nominated by their member states and appointed by the **Council of Europe** for four years. They remain in their regions and only get together for Committee meetings. Working at grass roots level, they are able to strengthen their region's links with European institutions by creating awareness, understanding and involvement in that region. They also advise and inform the European Parliament or the Council on regional matters. The Committee carries out research and produces studies of issues that affect the whole of Europe. For example, this could be a study of the quality of life in Europe's towns and regions. This is where the effects of membership of the EU are most often felt. Members of the Committee also work closely with the local and regional representatives of countries applying for membership of the EU, so that they are kept well informed and involved in the process.

Money for the regions

Councillor Colin Beardwood, Chairman of the West Midlands Regional Chamber declared:
'European support has provided a lifeline for many parts of the West Midlands region. It has helped hold together both urban and rural communities in difficult times.'

In 2005, the total EU **budget** was about 106 billion Euros. This comes from **tariffs** on goods entering the EU from outside and from contributions by member states. These contributions are basically worked out on a particular country's ability to pay. Some 35 per cent of EU spending, only slightly less on agriculture, goes on regional development.

EU leaders in discussion at the Maastricht Conference in 1991.

THE EU AND ITS CITIZENS
Regionalism in action

The European Regional Development Fund (ERDF) provides financial assistance to areas of economic decline, deprivation and disadvantage. How it operates is a good example of how the EU attempts to establish **cohesion** throughout the Community, whilst at the same time working closely with regional and local governments and business. It also shows the way in which EU money is carefully and precisely targeted. EU legislation identifies development areas in the member states and how funding should be allocated. The purpose of the Fund is **regeneration** and development. The addition of ten comparitively poor new member states in 2004 has called for a complete rethink of how regional development is handled, and this is currently under discussion.

The European Social Fund (ESF), another of the Structural Funds, supports some of the work of regeneration by, amongst other things, providing **vocational** training for young people in areas of long-term youth unemployment. This involves specific training using new technologies.

In recent years, European funding in the UK has included the following areas:

>> To help regions that are lagging behind other parts of the EU in terms of economic output. The funding enables affected areas to increase their ability to create wealth for their inhabitants. Areas that have received funding include Merseyside, South Yorkshire, the Highlands of Scotland, North and West Wales and Cornwall. Northern Ireland has received extra funding to support the peace process.

>> To support economic and social conversion of areas with structural problems. This might include an area where traditional industry has declined leaving high unemployment. Areas that receive this aid are divided into urban, rural, industrial and fisheries zones.

>> To support education, employment and training.

Since 2000, aid has also been provided under four EU community initiatives. These are known as:

>> INTEREG for cooperation between different regions

>> URBAN for urban development

>> LEADER for rural development

>> EQUAL to support initiatives that fight against racial and gender **discrimination** in employment.

Regional Development Agencies

These have been set up by the Government in the UK to develop plans to deal with structural problems and improve the economic performance of certain regions. There are nine of these agencies. The government funds them, but the agencies operate independently of it.

>>

Urban redevelopment

Liverpool and Merseyside are two areas that have long suffered as a result of economic and urban deterioration. High unemployment rates and **dereliction** are partly associated with the decline of its docklands and associated industries. A number of schemes have helped bring about growth and improvement. Redevelopment in the heart of Liverpool has done much to regenerate a once flagging business district. This redevelopment is funded collectively by the ERDF, Liverpool City Council and other business interests including the North West Regional Development Agency.

The terminal building of Speke Airport (now John Lennon airport) was redeveloped as a four-star hotel. During the 1980s, this building had become derelict. Built in 1937–40, this landmark, listed building is closely associated with people and events dear to the heart of the people of Liverpool – the Beatles, for example, and the football successes of Liverpool FC in the 1970s. Therefore, the importance of its regeneration was not just centred around the improvement of the environment and the creation of jobs.

Other projects have been undertaken in Liverpool, Knowsley and the Wirral involving the ERDF in partnership with regional organizations. These include:

>> Redevelopment of other industrial landmarks such as the Bryant and May match factory, built originally in 1918

>> Further development of business areas, office buildings and the public access to them

>> Conference and function facilities

>> A rail freight terminal

>> Development of derelict dockland into an industrial park.

>> A new rail link between John Lennon Airport and the city centre.

These projects have not only improved the environment and raised morale by removing the visible signs of decay, but have created thousands of jobs. Support for Merseyside continues, in spite of the fact that there are still areas yet to be redeveloped.

The John Lennon Airport redevelopment scheme has created a new, historically interesting hotel and preserved an important Liverpool landmark.

THE EU AND ITS CITIZENS
Regional development in Scotland, Wales and Northern Ireland

Scotland

Scotland has benefited from its association with the EU at a regional level. Funding has enhanced and developed almost every aspect of life in Scotland – large and small businesses, **import** and **export** trade, urban redevelopment, **diversification** in the agricultural and fishing industries, education and the promotion of Scotland's distinctive culture including support for the development of the Gaelic language. Support has also come for less populated areas, especially the Western Isles. During the period 2000–2006 the EU made € 319.80 available to boost the economy of the islands and the well being of its inhabitants in a variety of ways:

The European Regional Development Fund supports many regional development projects.

>> The development of business by the building of modern offices and a new industrial estate on Stornaway

>> Improving tourist attractions

>> Cultural and community facilities such as the new museum at Kildonan on South Uist. This development has been supported by the ERDF and has involved the conversion of an old school building into a museum complex including a café, rehearsal room, workshop and display area. It is also a centre for the island's local history and crafts.

>> Developments in remote areas, such as the further education facility being provided for Benbecula, to enable access to further education and training provided by Lews Castle College and the University of the Highlands.

European Regional Development Fund (ERDF)

>>

Wales

The Welsh people have welcomed the opportunity that European funding has created to provide Wales with the prospect of economic growth, as its agriculture and industry have been severely depressed. Action in Wales, as elsewhere, is based on partnerships between the EU and organizations in the public, private and voluntary sector. All schemes are approved by the National Assembly for Wales and the European Commission. Between 2000 and 2006, schemes tackled:

>> The redevelopment of industrial and rural areas that are declining

>> Solutions to long-term unemployment especially of the young

>> The redevelopment of rural Wales involving, for example, the development of tourism, and the processing and marketing of agricultural products

>> Developments in depressed urban areas.

This involved small, local projects as well as larger initiatives involving a variety of partners. The Coalfields Regeneration Trust established in 1999 is one example of such a partner. Its purpose is to address the hardships faced by coalmining communities following pit closures and the subsequent high unemployment. It aims to support the redevelopment of communities and encourage them to become independent. One example is Groundwork Wrexham, an environmental project, designed to provide the support people in the coalfield communities needed to become involved in making their own surroundings better.

Northern Ireland

The EU has been especially supportive of the peace process in Northern Ireland. Besides supporting the **regeneration** of the economy, it is concerned with creating more harmony in the country through employment programmes and increased prosperity. Through a body called Cooperation Ireland, the EU funds measures to encourage the development of cross-border links and projects, both economic and social. For example:

>> The Cross Border Community Development Project is based in Monaghan. It aims to create cross-border projects between community groups.

>> A Community Resource Centre has been set up on the Tullacmongan housing estate in Cavan Town. Families migrated and settled here from the north of Ireland when the violence there was at its worst. The centre has been provided to deal with the social and economic problems that were caused because of this. It is succeeding in bringing people together and in creating a community spirit that had previously not existed.

Celtic Knots

Another interesting collaborative project funded by the EU is Celtic Knots. This involves Irish and Welsh partners in a scheme to provide on-board training to staff working on the new ferries operating across the Irish Sea.

THE EU AND ITS CITIZENS
Citizens of Europe on the move

One of the great benefits that you can enjoy as a European **citizen** is the freedom to travel throughout the member states of the EU without any problems. You also have the opportunity to live, to work, to study and to be involved in sporting activities anywhere in Europe. How has this come about?

Goods on the move

It began with the **Treaty of Rome** (see pages 10–11). In 1957, this established a '**common market**' based on the idea that economic recovery and prosperity would be helped if there were greater, unrestricted, movement of people and goods around Europe. Trade would prosper if there were no barriers between countries to prevent the free flow of goods and services. At the basis of the 'common market', there were four 'freedoms':

>> Free movement of goods

>> Free movement of capital (money)

>> Freedom to provide services, for example, insurance and banking

>> Free movement of people.

So was born the idea of a single European market giving national businesses access to a huge European market. You only have to look at the large number of goods you can buy from the EU in your local supermarket to appreciate the difference that this has made. It also helped to break down the hostile barriers that previously arose when individual countries charged high **import** taxes (**tariffs**) on foreign goods entering the country.

People on the move

The free movement of people across the EU is essential to the success of the single market. Free movement brings with it a new range of cultural, educational and economic opportunities, and many of the EU states agreed to remove their border controls under the 'Schengen Agreement'. In the early years, great emphasis was placed on the free movement of workers but recently, more focus has been placed on students and retired people being able to travel easily. Since 1995, over 830,000 young people from across the EU have studied, trained or worked in another member state with support from Commission sponsored education and youth programmes (see the Find Out box).

Currently, EU citizens may live anywhere in the Union on two conditions. These are:

>> They must be covered by sickness insurance

>> They must also be receiving welfare benefits or have sufficient income 'to avoid becoming a burden on the social assistance system of the host member state'.

Sport on the move

On 27 April 2001, the Dutch footballer, Ruud van Nistelrooy, transferred from PSV Eindhoven to Manchester United for a record-breaking fee of £19 million. British football teams now have countless numbers of European players, just as British players take up profitable transfers to European clubs. This easy, two-way flow would have been extremely difficult in the days before the EU. Similarly, fans from Britain and all over Europe have the opportunity to support their teams wherever they play. The 2004 European Cup finals in Portugal showed how freedom of movement within the EU has made this possible. Sport is helping to create a sense of being 'European' although, sadly, incidents of football hooliganism, violence and racism suggest that there is still some way to go. Sport can bring out the best and the worst in people. It brings people together, but its also divides as competition sometimes assumes national, rather than team, rivalry (that is to say, you are supporting your own country rather than just a team). The massive police and security operations that accompany international football events may be an unhappy reminder of this but are not, in themselves, regarded as a reason to prevent people from attending such events. The Council of Europe remains committed to 'Sport for All'. Successful international rugby, golf, athletics and equestrian events show how this belief can succeed.

Dutch footballer Ruud van Nistelrooy with manager Sir Alex Ferguson on the day he joined English Premiership football club Manchester United.

FIND OUT... 🔍 ≫

The EU has been active in developing high quality programmes of education and vocational training. An important part of this has been the deliberate policy of removing obstacles, practical, legal and linguistic, to movement around the EU. One of these initiatives is the *Socrates programme*. This provides funding for individuals at all levels and stages of the educational process to study abroad, so sharing and exchanging ideas and experiences. It brings together young citizens from the 25 member states, with their hugely diverse cultures and political backgrounds. The programme is now in its second phase (2000–2006) and is funded by € 1,850 million. You can discover more about this at http://europa.eu.int/comm/education/socrates.html

THE EU AND ITS CITIZENS
Freedom at a price?

The freedom of movement and of opportunity in the EU is obviously welcome. On the other hand, it can be argued that removing the barriers that divided the countries of Europe has meant removing the barriers that also protected us. It has potentially assisted the growth of international, organized crime on a huge scale, encouraging such things as:

>> Drug trafficking

>> Vice and pornography

>> Stolen vehicles and goods

>> Illegal **immigration** rackets

>> **Money laundering**

>> Terrorism

Of course, all these things already existed, but border controls made this kind of illegal activity more difficult to operate. Maintaining freedom of movement, therefore, means preventing this kind of crime in other ways. The EU responded to this need in 1994 when **Europol** was set up under the terms of the

Maastricht Treaty to deal specifically with the crimes listed above. Europol's function is to ensure that information about national or international criminal activity is given to member nations quickly. It is not a police force. It does not have the authority to arrest or hold suspects. It has strict regulations about the collection and storage of data to safeguard the rights and freedom of innocent individuals or organizations.

Europol's success depends on the cooperation of police and Customs officials in all the member states. The Europol Convention of 1995 came into full force in 1998 when it was **ratified** by all the member countries. Under the terms of this convention, all member countries have their own Europol National Unit. In Britain, this is the National Criminal Intelligence Service (NCIS), set up in 1996 by the Home Secretary at that time, Jack Straw. Each

Europol can provide information to help customs in drug seizures, like this haul of heroin, worth £15 million.

>>

National Unit is expected to provide information to the law enforcement bodies of member countries, on request and quickly. This is vital in tracking people suspected of criminal activity, as they move freely around Europe. By 1999, Europol's role also included action to prevent terrorism. Representatives of national law enforcement bodies (Europol Liaison Officers) make up the Europol Management Board that is based at its headquarters in The Hague (Netherlands). In the days before the EU and Europol, criminals crossing international borders were almost beyond the reach of any authorities. This is no longer the case.

Europol in action

There are now many recent examples of international cooperation with Europol to deal with organized crime. In 1997, for example, an investigation into drug trafficking in Sweden (Operation Carl) involved the active cooperation of national Europol units in Belgium, Denmark, Spain, Germany and the Netherlands in tracking the network of people involved in the trafficking. As a result, huge quantities of drugs were seized. Similarly, 170 kg of heroin has recently been seized as a result of international cooperation – Operation Pristina – involving nine EU member states and six others. A criminal organization based in Pristina, in Kosovo, was trafficking drugs all over Europe. This time it was the Italian authorities that asked for Europol's support. Up to now, there have been 40 arrests and the investigation is ongoing.

Operation Primo is a good example of the importance of international cooperation. It also illustrates the problems caused by the ability to move easily around Europe. The operation began in 1997, when the Italian authorities discovered a house where drugs smuggled from the Netherlands were being stored. Investigations soon revealed that the same group of people connected with this house were being investigated separately by the police in several EU countries, and were involved in drug trafficking in Thailand, Hong Kong, Brazil, Argentina, Bolivia, Holland, Germany and Italy. Only when police began to work together and Europol national units supplied information to their central Department of Analysis did they begin to get results. The rapid spread of information between the EU member states led to twenty arrests. The focal point of this criminal operation supplying drugs was a German national, born in Poland and living in Amsterdam.

Following the terrorist attacks on New York in 2001, an anxious Europol increased the resources available to its Counter-Terrorism Unit. Expansion continued after the Madrid bombings of March 2004 and a Counter-Terrorism Task Force was established within the Counter-Terrorism Unit. Europol assisted the Metropolitan Police after the London bombings of July 2005 and, after the failed attacks of 21 July, it helped trace would-be bombers who had fled the UK. The arrest of terrorist suspect Osman Hussein in Rome on 30 July 2005 showed just how vital trans-European policing is.

THE EU AND ITS CITIZENS
Diversity in Europe

The EU is built on the idea that by living and working together and through cooperation, Europe can become a better place to live. The many differences between the peoples of Europe are seen as the EU's strengths and not its weaknesses – provided that these differences are respected.

Every country in the EU has its own history, its own language and its own national culture. These factors, together with others, have obviously influenced the characters and attitudes of the people living in these countries. Some member states like the United Kingdom, France and the Netherlands, have had a history of groups of immigrants settling in the country, and influencing its development. In the United Kingdom, for example, there are large Asian, African and West Indian communities, all of which have made a great contribution to the economic and cultural development of our country. The same is true of the North African communities in France.

The diversity between the peoples of Europe can be seen in a variety of ways:

>> Foods available in markets, local shops and supermarkets

>> Restaurants

>> Places of religious worship

>> Written and verbal languages

>> Types of music and dress

>> Clothes and fashion

>> Buildings – houses and streets

>> Appearance and physical characteristics.

People often find it difficult to accept the differences between peoples, both in their own countries and across Europe. British visitors to Europe, particularly for the first time, find some customs difficult to understand. Some find ordering food in restaurants difficult, whilst the custom of shops and banks closing around noon each day for as long as three hours can be both confusing and frustrating. In most cases, these are relatively small differences and can be resolved fairly easily. As British people visit Europe more and more, these differences will seem to be less important. In the same way, the customs traditional in the United Kingdom will become more understandable to European visitors.

However, the failure to understand and appreciate the differences between people can have more sinister outcomes – particularly when it leads to racism. If certain people focus on the differences between people over their colour, race and religion, racism can result. The most graphic and horrifying example of this is the treatment of Jews in Nazi Germany, 1933–1945. Hitler and the Nazis used traditional beliefs about Jews to blame them for all

>>

Germany's problems, from defeat in World War I to high unemployment. They created in Germany an environment that accepted **discrimination** against Jews, and their ill treatment, as both natural and a good thing. The horrifying end result was the killing of six million European Jews at Nazi hands in what is known as the Holocaust.

Those who believe in peace and in the idea of different peoples living together in harmony regard racism with suspicion and concern. Following the Madrid and London bombings of 2004 and 2005, aggresive behaviour towards Europe's Muslim communities increased. Many were wrongly categorised as accomplices to terrorism just because of their faith or the colour of their skin. At the same time, workers from former communist states were abused for seeking jobs in Western Europe. These are just two of the important issues facing the

French right-wing politician Jean Marie Le Pen attracted widespread support by airing views many found disturbingly racist.

EU today – both must be swiftly settled if further violence is to be avoided.

The European Monitoring Centre on Racism and **Xenophobia** was set up in 1997 by the EU to help to combat racism, xenophobia and **anti-Semitism** across Europe. It works with the Council of Europe and the **United Nations** to keep track of incidents of racism in Europe. All this information is then stored on a central network for distribution to those groups trying to combat racist and anti-Semitic material.

FIND OUT... 🔍 ≫

Sometimes people are discriminated against because of different ethnic or national backgrounds. Why do you think that some people are racist? What actions can you take to try and stop racism? What different ethnic, cultural, linguistic or religious groups can you find in your local area?

Some young people recently suggested that a motto for Europe could be 'UNITY IN DIVERSITY'. What do you think of this as a motto? What would be your motto?

THE EU AND ITS CITIZENS
Sustainable development

It can be argued that, in so many ways, the policies and actions of the organization that we call the EU provides us with an idea of at least some of the values and attitudes basic in responsible citizenship. It does much, for example, to promote tolerance, support fundamental **human rights**, and to oppose **discrimination** by race and gender. Responsible citizenship also involves stewardship – that is preserving and conserving our world for future generations. It also implies the need to provide a more 'comfortable' present and a future for the poorer parts of the world and their inhabitants. This is what is meant by sustainable development. EU involvement in these issues also helps to develop our understanding of global citizenship.

What is sustainable development?

Sustainable development is development that meets the needs of people in the present without affecting the ability of future generations to meet their own needs. It contains within it two key concepts:

>> The concept of needs, in particular the essential needs of the world's poor, to which total priority should be given

>> The idea of limitations imposed by the state of technology and social organization on the environment's ability to meet present and future needs.

We all know of the environmental dangers threatening our planet – rapid global warming produced by the 'greenhouse effect', the reduction of the ozone layer, pollution from waste, the devastation of the rain forests and, of course, the ever-present threat of nuclear pollution and devastating accidents such as that at Chernobyl, Ukraine in 1986, when a nuclear reactor exploded, leaking lethal radiation into the atmosphere. Young people are amongst the most active in promoting 'green' policies, encouraging recycling and biodegradable products (those that rot away naturally, without causing the environment any harm) as well as supporting projects to meet the needs of the developing world. But what is the European Community doing to ensure sustainable development?

The EU first incorporated sustainable development in its areas for action in 1987. Now these issues form a fundamental part of its work. The EU is taking action in the five major environmental areas that have been identified as priorities for international action. These are: climate change, **biodiversity**, forests, the ozone layer and **desertification**.

The EU has launched a series of environmnetal Action Plans supported by hard-hitting directives and legal action against those who break them. By late 2004, 507 cases were being prosecuted. The Action Plans include the following:

>> Insisting on comprehensive recycling of waste materials

>> Setting targets and developing policies for EU members to reduce emissions of greenhouse gases

>> Supporting developing countries in managing their natural resources

>> Helping to develop ways of managing tropical rain forests (for example, the Brazilian Pilot Programme, and the Philippines Integrated Protected Areas Programme)

>> Limiting desertification by encouraging local involvement in conservation schemes to keep soil fertile

>> Family planning and health education projects to prevent the over-population of poor and deprived areas

>> Schemes to preserve fish stocks and other forms of marine life from pollution.

Fossil-fuelled power stations and heavy industries continue to cause pollution in some parts of Europe.

European aid

The EU also provides aid to developing countries through the European Development Fund. Much of this aid is used to put into action the programmes discussed above. This is particularly true of funded projects in African, Caribbean, Asian and Latin American countries. Mediterranean countries are working in cooperation with the EU on schemes to protect the Mediterranean Sea from pollution. This includes a ban on ships dumping waste and other materials at sea. Changes in Central and Eastern Europe brought about by the collapse of **communism** have encouraged EU involvement to protect the environment and plan economic reform.

China and the EU

The EU has helped China combat its serious environmental problems. These include atmospheric pollution (China has nine out of the ten most polluted cities in the world) and water pollution resulting from excessive use of fertilizers and pesticides. Meeting in June 2005, EU Environment Commissioner Stavros Dimas and Chinese Environmnet Minister Xie Zenhua declared they were in agreement over air pollution, bio-diversity and climate change. Time alone will tell.

THE EU AND ITS CITIZENS
Facing the future
Economic and Monetary Union (EMU)

The EU is at an important point in its history. Two major challenges face the Union and its member states. The controversies surrounding the **Euro** and Economic and **Monetary** Union (EMU) are possibly the most serious. The Euro is the name of the proposed single **currency** for the EU.

On 1 January 1999, the Euro became the official currency of twelve of fifteen member states of the EU – Austria, Belgium, Finland, France, Germany, Greece, Ireland, Italy, Luxembourg, Netherlands, Portugal and Spain. Between January 1999 and the end of 2001, the Euro and existing national currencies, like the French Franc, operated together. The year 2002 saw these national currencies of participating member states ceasing to be legal tender.

Not all EU members agreed with the single currency. Denmark opted out and Sweden also refused to participate. The UK government welcomed the idea in principle but was a long way off joining.

Britain and the single currency

Arguments in favour:

>> Since the single market is such an important part of the EU, it seems sensible for it to have one single currency, rather than as many as 28 different national currencies!

>> The Central European Bank is already setting a common interest rate within the Eurozone and the UK cannot afford to be left out.

Arguments against:

>> If the United Kingdom accepts Economic and Monetary Union and joins the Euro, it will remove our freedom to run our own economy

>> The Euro has had serious teething problems, with major nations unable to abide by the regulations of the European Central Bank.

>> Most important of all, those who oppose a single currency and EMU do so because they believe that more power will pass from our British Parliament to Europe and we will become part of a large and centralized European state.

This issue goes to the heart of the EU and its future. Some Britons are happy with the EU as it is – a largely trading venture – while others wish to see its member states grow even closer together until a federal Europe is established. The current debate about the Euro, therefore, is not just about a single currency – it is also about how the EU will develop in the future.

Where now?

In February 2002, EU officials began writing a formal constitution for their organization. It was planned as a tidying up exercise, clarifying several overlapping treaties and setting down what the EU really was. In June 2004, Europe's heads of state finally agreed on the constitution's wording. All that was needed was formal agreement by the 25 states within two years. The formality, however, became a nightmare.

Each country chose its own process. In Belgium, for instance, Parliament made the formal agreement, while the British government decided on a referendum of all voters. Several states, including Slovenia and Spain, soon made their formal agreement. Then, on 29 May 2005, came the bombshell: France, a vital player in the European movement since its beginnig, rejected the constitution in its referendum. The Dutch soon followed suit and other states, including Britain, put their plans on hold. What had gone wrong? Here are some suggestions:

French campaigners protested strongly against the European Constitution.

>> Voters used constitutional referendums to show dissatisfaction with their nation governments, not with the EU

>> Europeans felt that the EU was not democratic enough

>> Rejection of the constitution revealed cracks within the EU that had been long covered up

>> EU leaders had forged ahead with their plans without convincing the public.

The rejection of the constitution presented the EU with a major crisis. How it is resolved will determine the institution's future for years to come.

FIND OUT...

The Young European Movement is Britain's pro-European youth organization. The organization's website is at www.euromove.org.uk/yem

FURTHER RESOURCES

National Representation in the European Parliament			
Member state	No. of MEPs	Member state	No. of MEPs
Austria	18	Latvia	9
Belgium	24	Lithuania	13
Cyprus	6	Luxemburg	6
Czech Republic	24	Malta	5
Denmark	14	Netherlands	27
Estonia	6	Poland	54
Finland	14	Portugal	24
France	78	Slovakia	14
Germany	99	Slovenia	7
Greece	24	Spain	54
Hungary	24	Sweden	19
Ireland	13	United Kingdom	78
Italy	78	Total	732

There are many different places to get more information about the European Union. Below are details of some of the best.

Useful websites

www.euromove.org.uk
the European Movement

europarl.eu.int
the European Parliament

www.fco.gov.uk
the Foreign Office

www.jef-europe.org
Young European Federalists

yem@euromove.org.uk
Young European Movement

www.polis.net
European political news and links

www.ecb.int
European Central Bank

www.hansard-society.org.uk
Hansard Society

www.coe.fr
Council of Europe

europa.eu.int
Official EU website

www.euroguide.org
Comprehensive detail

Useful addresses

European Commission
8 Storey's Gate
London
SW1P 3AT

European Parliament
2 Queen Anne's Gate
London
SW1H 9AA

Young European Movement
FREEPOST SW 287
London SW1W 9ZZ

Further reading

The Government and Politics of the European Union, fourth edition, by Neill Nugent. UK: Palgrave, formerly Macmillan Press, 1999.

Understanding the European Union, by John McCormick. UK: Palgrave, formerly Macmillan Press, 1999.

The European Union: a Very Short Introduction, by John Pinder. UK: Oxford Paperbacks, 2001.

The UK & the Euro, by P Temperton. UK: John Wiley and Sons Ltd, 2001.

GLOSSARY

accountable	answerable for one's actions, e.g. to Parliament or to the electors
anti-Semitism	prejudice or hostility towards Jews
Berlin Wall	a symbol of the division of Europe during the Cold War. It came down in November, 1989.
biodiversity	a range of living things in a particular environment
budget	the EU spends about £60 billion each year. The average net contribution from Britain is about £30 per person. About half the budget is spent on the Common Agricultural Policy.
Charter of Fundamental Human Rights	the idea that EU treaties should state the rights of citizens to be respected throughout the EU
citizens	ordinary people within the EU – their status was first introduced in the Maastricht Treaty
civil servants	employees of the civil service – all government departments other than the armed forces
cohesion	the idea that the poorer regions of the EU should be given help in improving their economies to help them catch up with the richer parts
Committee of the Regions	a body of the EU which represents regional and local government and which is consulted on legislation
Common Market	another way of referring to the EU
Commonwealth	a group of countries that used to be part of the British Empire and still retain some links with the UK
communism	a social and political system in which property is owned by the community and each member works for the common benefit
constituency	an area in which the voters elect a representative
constituents	voters who elect someone to represent them
consultative	refers to the process of consulting – asking people their views about an issue
consumers	a person who buys or uses goods and services
Council of Europe	separate from the EU, based in Strasbourg. It deals with issues such as human rights.
currency	money in use in a country
customs duty	money charged on goods imported from other countries
damages	money paid or claimed as compensation for an injury
dereliction	abandoned, run down
desertification	making or becoming a desert
directive	an instruction issued by those in authority
discrimination	unfair treatment based on prejudice, e.g. sexual or racial
diversify, diversification	introduce variety, widen out
ECU	European Currency Unit
EEC	European Economic Community – the old name for the European Union
Euro	the new single currency of the EU which has replaced the national currencies of eleven member states
European Commission	the equivalent of the government in a member state. It has 20 Commissioners.
European Council	a meeting of the heads of the national governments held normally every six months

Europol	a body that coordinates international police cooperation in the EU – based in The Hague
exchange rate	the value of one currency in terms of another
export	sending goods to another country for sale
federal, federalism	the opposite of nationalism with more power given to the European Parliament
human rights	rights held to belong to a person, e.g. the right to vote
import	to bring into a country for the purpose of sale
industrialization	the process of becoming industrial, e.g. a country changing from an agricultural to an industrial one
Maastricht Treaty	agreed at the end of 1991 – it transformed the European Community into the European Union
monetary	the currency of a country – its monetary system
money laundering	transfer of money to conceal its origins
nationalism	the idea that there should be no international restrictions on how a country is governed – the opposite of federalism
ombudsman	an official appointed to investigate complaints by individuals against public authorities, e.g. governments
passport controls	using passports to control the movement of people into and out of a country
proportional representation	an electoral system in which each party has a number of seats in proportion to the number of votes for its candidates
qualified majority voting	used in the Council of Ministers to decide on such matters as commercial policy. There is no veto.
quotas	the maximum number or amount of people or things that may be admitted to a country or institution
ratify	to give formal consent to something
referendum	a fairly common way for a member state to decide European issues. Questions are decided by the people rather than by the government.
regeneration	give new life or vigour
resources	available assets, the wealth of a country
set aside	the method used in farming of 'setting aside' land, i.e not using it to produce crops, often to reduce the amount produced
single market	a free market among all EU member states
subsidies	grants paid to an industry or cause needing help, or to keep down the price at which goods are sold
tariff	duty to be paid on imports or exports
trade unions	associations of employees engaged in a particular type of work, formed to protect their rights and interests
treaties	a word used to describe, for example, the Treaty of Rome and the Maastricht and Amsterdam Treaties
Treaty of Amsterdam	the latest set of reforms to the various treaties – agreed in 1997
Treaty of Rome	signed in 1957, it created the European Economic Community
unanimous	all agreeing on an opinion or decision
United Nations	organization of over 150 countries set up in 1945 to promote world peace
veto	the power that each member state has to prevent a decision being reached in the Council of Ministers
vocational	directed to a particular job or career
xenophobia	hatred or distrust of foreigners

INDEX